23 Ready-To-Go Lesson Plans

LANGUAGE ARTS

GRADE 3

What Are Lifesaver Lessons®?

Lifesaver Lessons® are everything you need to deliver a well-planned lesson at a moment's notice. Lifesaver Lessons are curriculum-based lesson plans that include:

- Simple preparations and materials needed
- Ideas for introducing the lessons
- Reproducible activities
- Extension ideas
- Patterns, awards, and booklists

www.themailbox.com

Project Editor:
Cynthia Holcomb

Writers:
Cynthia Holcomb, Nicole Iacovazzi,
Susan Kotchman, Cheryl Stickney

Artists:
Jennifer Tipton Bennett,
Cathy Spangler Bruce,
Clevell Harris, Rob Mayworth,
Donna K.Teal

Cover Artist:
Jennifer Tipton Bennett

Lifesaver Lessons®

Table Of Contents

©1997 by THE EDUCATION CENTER, INC.
All rights reserved.
ISBN# 1-56234-170-7

Manufactured in the United States
10 9 8 7 6 5 4 3

A "Bee" C

Your students will be all a-buzz with this honey of a lesson to reinforce alphabetizing skills.

Skill: Alphabetizing to the third letter

Estimated Lesson Time: 30 minutes

Teacher Preparation:
Duplicate page 5 for each student.

Materials:
1 copy of page 5 per student

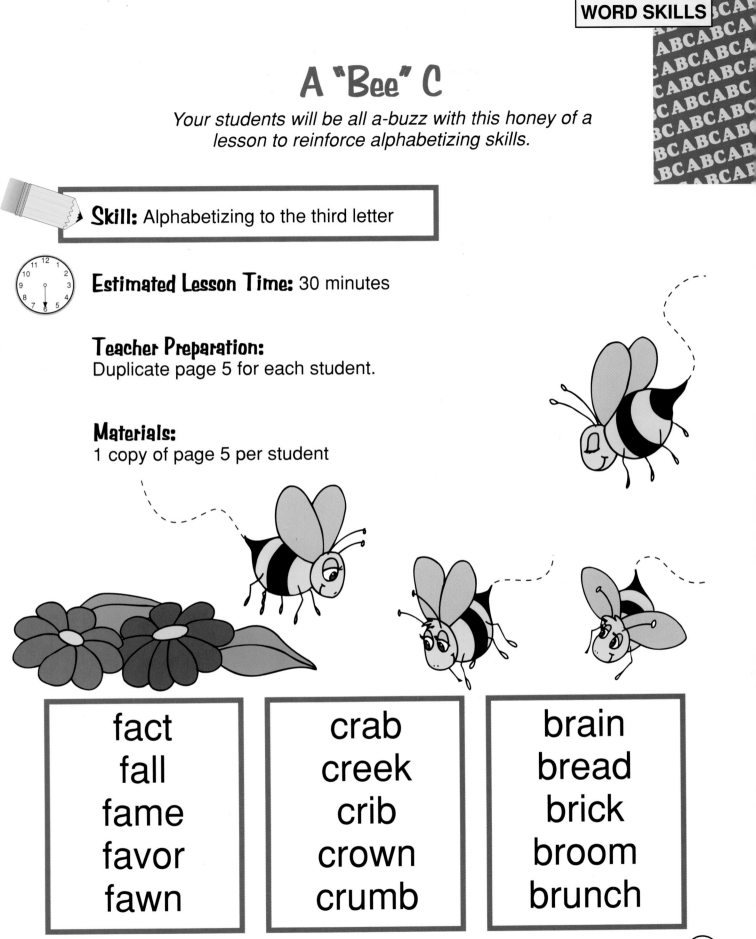

fact	crab	brain
fall	creek	bread
fame	crib	brick
favor	crown	broom
fawn	crumb	brunch

Introducing The Lesson:

Ask students to think of words that begin with the letter *b*. List the responses on the board and have students arrange the words in alphabetical order. Then tell students that they will "bee" on a mission to get some hives in order.

Steps:

1. Review rules for alphabetizing to the third letter.

2. Distribute a copy of page 5 to each student.

3. Pair students together to check their answers.

4. Challenge students to complete the Bonus Box activity.

baby	best	block	brown
back	big	blue	brush
ball	bike	boat	bump
bat	bill	boss	bunch
beach	bird	bow	bus
bell	black	brave	buzz
bench	blend	bright	

Name _____ *Alphabetizing*

A "Bee" C

Arrange the words buzzing around each bee in alphabetical order.
Write the words in ABC order on the hives.

smoke

smudge

smear

smart

smile

great

grill

growl

grape   grudge

enclose   engine

enjoy

enough   enter

blend   blow

blush   black   blind

cloud   climb

club

clever   class

©1997 The Education Center, Inc. • *Lifesaver Lessons*™ • Grade 3 • TEC494 • Key p. 95

How To Extend The Lesson:

- Have students make an alphabetized list of foods on the daily lunch menu.

- Divide the class into two groups and have each group alphabetize the titles of their library books.

- Ask each student to choose a crayon from his box; then have students line up in alphabetical order according to the color names of their crayons.

- List the names of five stores on the board. Have students work in pairs to look up the store names in the phone book.

- Have students brainstorm a list of items that contain alphabetized information, or places where alphabetical order is used to organize materials.

- Program copies of the patterns below with vocabulary words. Place the patterns in a center. Encourage each student to visit the center and arrange the words in alphabetical order.

Patterns

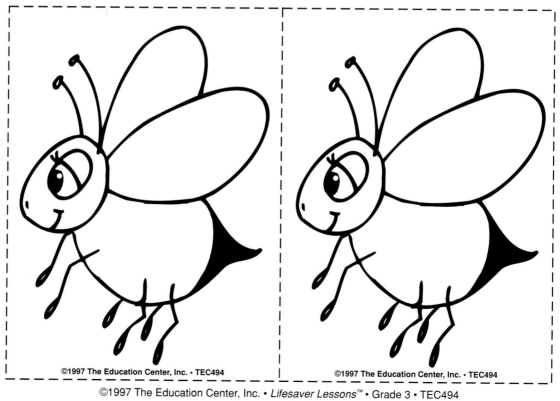

©1997 The Education Center, Inc. • TEC494   ©1997 The Education Center, Inc. • TEC494

In Search Of Suffixes

*Turn your students into supersleuths with this activity
to track down suffixes!*

Skill: Recognizing suffixes

Estimated Lesson Time: 40 minutes

Teacher Preparation:
1. Duplicate page 9 for each student.
2. Gather several newspapers, enough for each student to have her own section.

Materials:
1 copy of page 9 per student
newspapers
scissors
glue

Background Information:
A *suffix* is an affix added to the end of a word or stem, forming a new word or an inflectional ending.

Suffix	Meaning
-able, -ible	able to, capable of
-ance, -ence, -ancy, -ency	quality, act, or condition
-ar, -er, -or	one who does something
-er, -est	superlative adjective
-ful	full of
-fy	to form into or become
-hood	state of being, membership in a group
-ing	gerund form of a verb, can form nouns from verbs
-ion, -sion, -tion	act, process, or condition
-ish	nationality, having likeness to
-ive	having the quality of, tending to
-less	without
-like	similar to
-ly	in a certain manner
-ment	result of, action or process
-ness	manner or state of being
-ward	toward, in the direction of
-wise	way, direction
-y, -ey	quality or state of

Introducing The Lesson:

Tell your detectives that they are going to go on a newspaper scavenger hunt to search for certain suffixes. Review the definitions of suffixes, focusing on *-ful, -less, -ing, -ly,* and *-ment.* Explain that each student is to look in the newspaper for words containing those suffixes. When a word is found, the student cuts and pastes it under the appropriate column on page 9.

Steps:

1. Distribute a copy of page 9 to each student.

2. Provide each student with newspapers, scissors, and glue.

3. Instruct students to search through the newspapers for words that contain the suffixes shown at the top of page 9.

4. Tell students to cut and paste the identified suffixes in the appropriate columns on page 9.

5. Provide students with a given amount of time to complete the activity. Then challenge them to complete the Bonus Box activity.

Recognizing suffixes

In Search Of...Suffixes

Look through newspapers for words that contain the suffixes shown below. Cut and paste each word in the correct column.

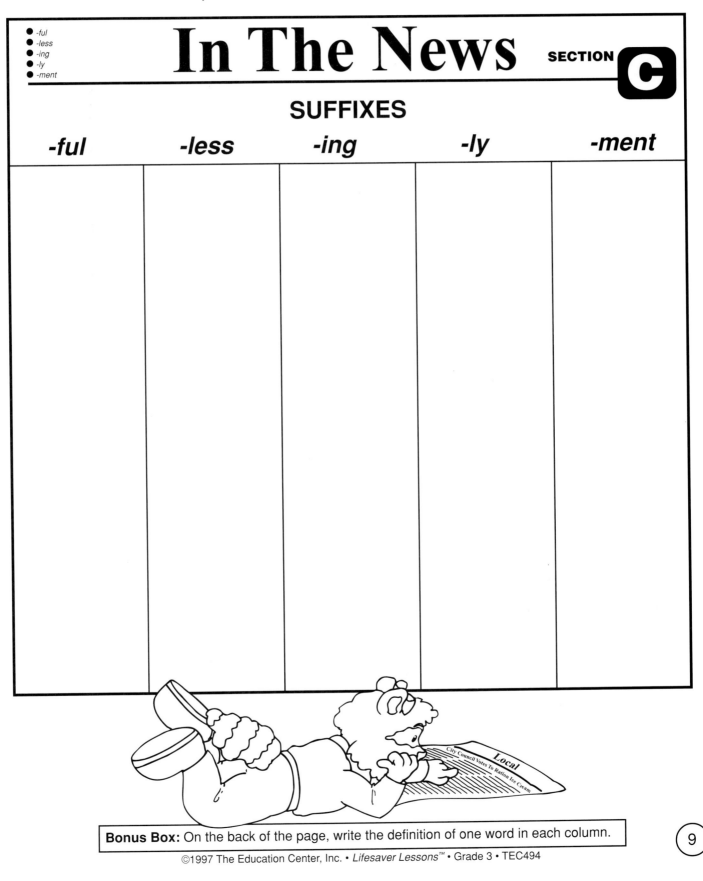

- -ful
- -less
- -ing
- -ly
- -ment

In The News   SECTION C

SUFFIXES

-ful	-less	-ing	-ly	-ment

Bonus Box: On the back of the page, write the definition of one word in each column.

How To Extend The Lesson:

• Have a pair of students read a storybook. Ask them to make a list of suffixes found in the story.

• Assign each student a suffix. Challenge him to list ten words that contain the suffix.

• Make a suffix dictionary. Have each student write a suffix, its meaning, and a sentence containing the word on a sheet of paper. Alphabetize the pages; then compile them into a class dictionary.

• Write a root word on the board. Challenge each student to list as many suffixes as possible that can be added to the word.

• Focus on one suffix each day. Ask students to be on the look-out for words containing the suffix, and keep a list of their discoveries on the board.

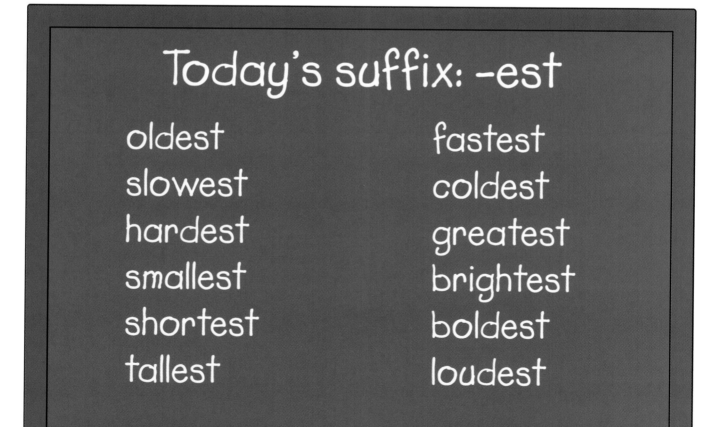

Today's suffix: -est

oldest	fastest
slowest	coldest
hardest	greatest
smallest	brightest
shortest	boldest
tallest	loudest

Just What The Doctor Ordered!

*This prescription for abbreviations will provide students
with a healthy dose of practice.*

Skill: Identifying abbreviations

Estimated Lesson Time: 30 minutes

Teacher Preparation:
1. Duplicate page 13 for each student.
2. Gather several student dictionaries.

Materials:
1 copy of page 13 per student
several student dictionaries

Teacher Reference:

a.m.	before noon	Mt.	Mountain
appt.	appointment	p.m.	after noon
apt.	apartment	pg.	page
Ave.	Avenue	vocab.	vocabulary
Blvd.	Boulevard	ASAP	as soon as possible
Co.	Company	ID	identification
dept.	department	IOU	I owe you
Dr.	Doctor	MPH	miles per hour
Hwy.	Highway	TV	television
Mr.	Title for a man	VIP	very important person
Mrs.	Title for a married woman		

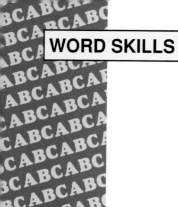

Introducing The Lesson:

Tell students that you are very tired today and you don't have much energy to write. On the board, write this sentence: "On Mon. we will read pg. 14 and answer the 2nd question." Ask students to identify the words that saved you energy in your writing.

Steps:

1. Have volunteers circle each abbreviation and then write the long form of each word.

2. Brainstorm with students a list of words that can be abbreviated. Record the words and the abbreviated spellings on the board.

3. Distribute a copy of page 13 to each student. Provide dictionaries for student reference.

4. Challenge students to complete the Bonus Box activity.

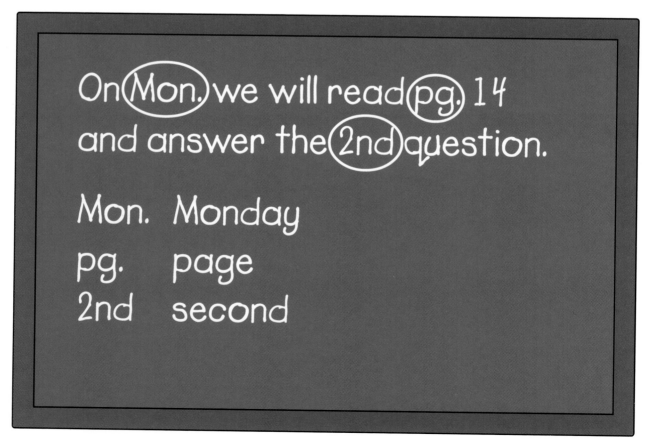

On (Mon.) we will read (pg.) 14 and answer the (2nd) question.

Mon.   Monday

pg.   page

2nd   second

Name_____

Just What The Doctor Ordered!

Read the paragraph and circle each abbreviation.
Then write the spelling of each abbreviated word.

   Last night I visited with Dr. Frederick Fungus, Jr., the most famous surgeon in the
U.S.A. He told me of a patient he treated last Tues. afternoon. Since Jan. 1st, the
patient had been having trouble with his hearing. After examining the patient,
Frederick found the problem. He rushed the man to the hospital E.R. on the corner
of Main St. and Pine Rd., where he pulled a meatball from the man's ear. The man
was very relieved. It was the 3rd time it had happened to him. He says it happens
every time he falls asleep while eating spaghetti.

abbreviation	complete spelling of word
1._____	_____
2._____	_____
3._____	_____
4._____	_____
5._____	_____
6._____	_____
7._____	_____
8._____	_____
9._____	_____
10._____	_____

Bonus Box: Create an abbreviation for the name of each person in your family.

How To Extend The Lesson:

- Have students look through the telephone book to find abbreviations. Challenge them to find and list at least ten.

- List some common abbreviated terms such as FBI, NBA, FYI, ASAP, and UFO. Have students guess what the acronyms stand for before you explain the meanings.

- Have students learn the abbreviations for the states. Introduce three or four abbreviations each day. Then quiz students in a spelling-bee-type contest to see who can identify the most states by their abbreviations.

- Tell each student to write a sentence. Then have him try to abbreviate several words in the sentence. Call on students to write their abbreviated sentences on the board for the class to try to decipher.

Alabama	AL	Kentucky	KY	North Dakota	ND
Alaska	AK	Louisiana	LA	Ohio	OH
Arizona	AZ	Maine	ME	Oklahoma	OK
Arkansas	AR	Maryland	MD	Oregon	OR
California	CA	Massachusetts	MA	Pennsylvania	PA
Colorado	CO	Michigan	MI	Rhode Island	RI
Connecticut	CT	Minnesota	MN	South Carolina	SC
Delaware	DE	Mississippi	MS	South Dakota	SD
District of Columbia	DC	Missouri	MO	Tennessee	TN
Florida	FL	Montana	MT	Texas	TX
Georgia	GA	Nebraska	NE	Utah	UT
Hawaii	HI	Nevada	NV	Vermont	VT
Idaho	ID	New Hampshire	NH	Virginia	VA
Illinois	IL	New Jersey	NJ	Washington	WA
Indiana	IN	New Mexico	NM	West Virginia	WV
Iowa	IA	New York	NY	Wisconsin	WI
Kansas	KS	North Carolina	NC	Wyoming	WY

Amazing Antonyms

Explore opposite words with this activity that promotes student individuality.

Skill: Using antonyms

Estimated Lesson Time: 30 minutes

Teacher Preparation:
1. Duplicate a copy of page 17 for each student.
2. Program pairs of index cards with opposite words. Prepare enough cards so that each student will have one.

Materials:
1 copy of page 17 per student
index cards programmed with antonyms

Background Information:
Antonyms are words with opposite meanings.

Teacher Reference:

above—below	crooked—straight	false—true	polite—rude
add—subtract	cry—laugh	forget—remember	poor—rich
alike—different	dangerous—safe	found—lost	right—wrong
asleep—awake	day—night	frown—smile	rough—smooth
backward—forward	deep—shallow	generous—selfish	save—spend
beautiful—ugly	destroy—repair	hard—soft	short—tall
begin—finish	difficult—easy	left—right	sour—sweet
believe—doubt	dry—wet	lose—win	tame—wild
big—small	early—late	noisy—quiet	terrible—wonderful
buy—sell	enemy—friend	over—under	whisper—yell
clean—dirty	fast—slow	play—work	

WORD SKILLS

Introducing The Lesson:

Begin this activity with a mixed-up matching game. Tell students that instead of playing a game where they find a matching pair of cards, they are to find cards that don't match; in fact, they must find cards that are complete opposites!

Steps:

1. Distribute an index card to each student. Instruct each student to find the person holding a card programmed with the opposite meaning from the word on his card. When students have paired up, have each pair announce the words on their cards. Explain that the term for an opposite word is *antonym.*

2. Distribute a copy of page 17 to each student.

3. Have each student complete the reproducible; then share the possible answers in a class discussion.

4. Challenge students to complete the Bonus Box activity.

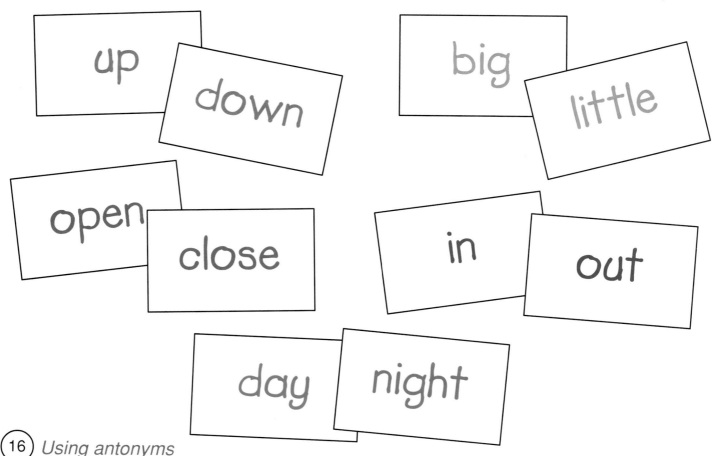

16 *Using antonyms*

Name _____

Amazing Antonyms
Complete each sentence with words that make the sentence true.

1. A _____ is cold, but a _____ is hot.

2. We see the _____ in the day, and the _____ at night.

3. A _____ is small, but a _____ is large.

4. _____ makes me happy, but _____ makes me sad.

5. A _____ is smooth, and a _____ is rough.

6. _____ is short, but _____ is tall.

7. I think _____ tastes good, and _____ tastes bad.

8. I like _____ in the summer, and _____ in the winter.

9. At my house, the _____ is empty, but the _____ is full.

10. A _____ is very slow, but a _____ is very fast.

Bonus Box: Underline the antonyms in each sentence.

©1997 The Education Center, Inc. • *Lifesaver Lessons* • Grade 3 • TEC494

17

How To Extend The Lesson:

- Write a character sketch on the board with a list of characteristics such as *tall, thin, kind, forgetful, likes to sing, runs quickly,* and *has an elephant.* Ask each student to write a description of a character who is the complete opposite of the one outlined on the board. Then have each student write a story using the two opposite characters.

- Have each student submit a paper with a paragraph telling about the best thing that has happened to him in third grade, and a paragraph telling about his worst third-grade experience. Compile student writing in a book titled "The Best And Worst Of Third Grade."

- Create an antonym list for several categories. Have students brainstorm animals that are considered opposites (such as a lion and a lamb, and a tortoise and a hare), time periods that are opposites (such as day and night, summer and winter, and a.m. and p.m.) and opposite words for these categories: action words, emotions, descriptions, and weather.

- Share these stories that have opposite themes with your students:
  —*Becca Backward, Becca Frontward: A Book Of Concept Pairs* by Bruce McMillan (Lothrop, Lee & Shepard; 1986)
  —*Fast-Slow, High-Low* by Peter Spier (Doubleday, 1988)
  —*Jethro And Joel Were A Troll* by Bill Peet (Houghton Mifflin Company, 1990)
  —*Red Cat, White Cat* by Peter Mandel (Henry Holt and Company, Inc.; 1994)
  —*Traffic: A Book Of Opposites* by Betsy Maestro and Giulio Maestro (Crown Books For Young Readers, 1991)

Weather
hot   cold
rainy   sunny
flood   drought

Feelings
cheerful   grumpy
helpful   bothersome
shy   bold

Actions
work   play
run   walk
cry   laugh

Time
dusk   dawn
evening   morning
night   day

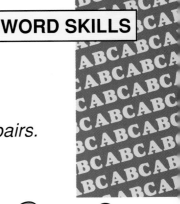

Two Scoops

Here's a tasty approach to reviewing homophone word pairs.

Skill: Discovering homophones

Estimated Lesson Time: 30 minutes

Teacher Preparation:
Duplicate page 21 for each student.

Materials:
1 copy of page 21 per student

Teacher Reference:

ate—eight	knight—night	sale—sail
be—bee	knot—not	sea—see
bear—bare	know—no	sew—so
blew—blue	knows—nose	some—sum
buy—by—bye	made—maid	son—sun
cents—scents—sense	male—mail	tail—tale
deer—dear	meat—meet—mete	there—their—they're
eye—I—aye	one—won	through—threw
hair—hare	pair—pear—pare	to—too—two
hear—here	plane—plain	way—weigh
hole—whole	principal—principle	week—weak
hour—our	red—read	would—wood
knew—new—gnu	road—rode	write—right—rite

Introducing The Lesson:

Tell students to close their eyes and picture an image for the sentence you are going to say out loud. When students have closed their eyes, say, "I ate one bowl of ice cream for breakfast." Have students open their eyes and describe the images they saw. Then write on the board "Eye eight won bowl of ice cream four breakfast." Ask students to proofread the sentence.

Steps:

1. Have student volunteers circle the words that are misspelled in the sentence.

2. Ask students to help you spell the correct form of each circled word. Discuss the word meanings of each homophone pair.

3. Distribute page 21 to each student.

4. Provide time for students to complete the homophone activity.

5. Challenge students to complete the Bonus Box activity.

Name _____

Two Scoops

Find the homonym pairs from the flavor list.
Write the pairs on the matching ice-cream cones.
Circle the word that is pictured on each cone.

Flavors
write
some
son
bare
deer
flour
would
knows
right
hair
sum
dear
flower
nose
hare
wood
sun
bear

1. $\dfrac{3}{7} = 4$

2.

3.

4.

5.

6.

7.

8.

9.

Bonus Box: Choose three homonym pairs. Write the meaning for each of the words on the back of this page.

How To Extend The Lesson:

- Place a supply of ice-cream scoop cutouts at a learning center. (See the patterns below.) Encourage students to think of homophone pairs and write each word of the pair on a scoop. Glue the scoops atop a cone-shaped cutout and staple the resulting ice-cream cone to a bulletin-board display.

- Use the ice-cream scoop patterns below to create a class supply of vocabulary cards. Program each scoop with the definition of one word in a homophone pair. Distribute a programmed scoop to each student. The student reads the definition and writes the word it defines on the back of the scoop. He then finds a student with a word that makes a homophone pair with his word. Have each student pair read their words and definitions to the class; then store the programmed scoops in a center for additional review.

- Initiate some wordplay into the classroom with this collection of books by Fred Gwynne. *A Little Pigeon Toad*, *A Chocolate Moose For Dinner*, and *The King Who Rained* (Simon and Schuster Children's Books, 1988) are full of humorous homophones, delightful double meanings, and clever illustrations. After sharing the books with your class, have students try their hands at creating plays on words.

Patterns

Focus On Following Directions

Students will learn the value of following directions with this activity that sharpens attention to detail.

Skill: Following written directions

Estimated Lesson Time: 20 minutes

Teacher Preparation:
Duplicate page 25 for each student.

Materials:
1 copy of page 25 per student

Following Directions Are Important When:

- Preparing a recipe
- Following safety procedures
- Assembling toys and other items
- Completing school assignments
- Taking medication
- Reading an instruction sheet
- Playing a game

Introducing The Lesson:

Ask students to brainstorm times when it is important to follow directions. Announce to your class that you have an important document that will assess each student's ability to follow written directions. The directions are not hard, but students will need to read carefully. As a pretest exercise, you will call out several directions, Simon Says style, to help students focus on paying attention to details.

Steps:

1. Call out several Simon Says directions, using instructions such as "Get out a pencil," "Put your feet flat on the floor," "Sit up straight," and "Read the directions on the upcoming paper carefully."

2. Distribute a copy of page 25 to each student. Remind students that the directions will be easy to follow, but should be read carefully.

3. Challenge students to complete the Bonus Box activity.

Simon says,
"Get out a pencil."

Simon says,
"Put your feet flat on the floor."

Stretch your arms
above your head.

Simon says,
"Sit up straight."

Wave your pencil in the air.

Simon says,
"Read the directions on the
upcoming paper carefully."

Name _____

Can You Follow Directions?

Read carefully to follow the directions on the page.

1. Read this entire list of directions before completing them.

2. Write your name at the top of the paper.

3. Put a star by your name at the top of the paper.

4. Circle the third word in this sentence.

5. Underline the last word in this sentence.

6. Color in all the *O*s in this sentence.

7. Cross out the second word in this sentence.

8. Draw a box around the shortest word in this sentence.

9. Turn the paper over and write your last name three times.

10. Now that you have finished reading all the directions, complete only number two. Then try the Bonus Box activity.

Bonus Box: On the back of this paper, make a list of jobs where it is not important to follow directions.

How To Extend The Lesson:

- Provide practice with listening skills by calling out a list of directions for students to follow. Instruct each student to complete such directions as writing her name in the upper left corner of her paper, writing the date in the lower left corner, drawing a tree in the center of the paper, and other simple instructions.

- Emphasize the importance of giving directions as well as following them. Have each student write a list of directions for preparing an easy snack, such as peanut butter and crackers. After he completes his list, let each student prepare the snack according to his directions. Help the student revise his directions if any key information was left out.

- Play a game of Simon Says to sharpen listening skills. Incorporate content review into the directions, such as "Simon says to show 18 minus 13 fingers," or "Simon says to face north."

- Combine listening skills and following directions with math practice. Call out a series of numbers and operations for students to write down. (For example, "Three plus five times two minus four.") Allow time for students to work the problem; then award a token for each correct response.

Tokens

Give The Main Idea A Hand!

Students will learn to state the main idea of any story with this helping hand!

 Skill: Determining the main idea

Estimated Lesson Time: 30 minutes

Teacher Preparation:
1. Duplicate page 29 for each student.
2. Select a story the class has read together.

Materials:
1 copy of page 29 per student
1 story the class has read together

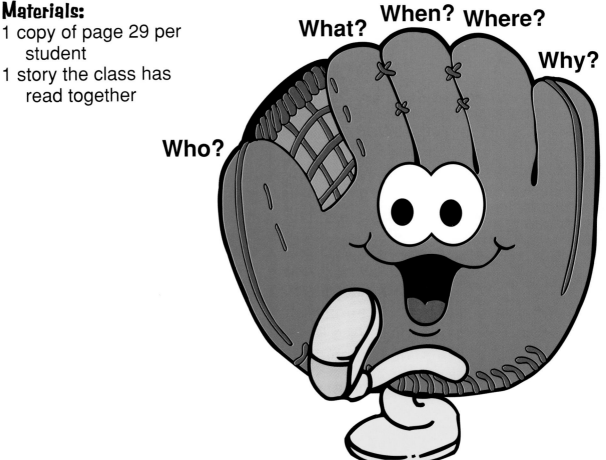

What? When? Where? Why? Who?

Determining the main idea (27)

Introducing The Lesson:

Announce to students that you have a piece of special equipment to help locate the main idea of any story. Tell them that you are going to show them the equipment and demonstrate the proper technique for using it. Then you will allow each student to practice using the equipment to locate the main idea of a story.

Steps:

1. Make a great fanfare of holding up your hand, showing students the front and back, and then drawing the outline of a hand on the board.

2. Tell students that to use the special equipment (the hand) they must remember to use each and every part (point to the fingers on the drawing). Each part will reveal an important piece of the main-idea statement.

3. Label the fingers on the hand diagram as follows: "when," "where," "who," "what," and "why." Tell students that when all of the pieces are put together, the main-idea statement is revealed.

4. Lead your students through a practice story such as *Little Red Riding Hood.* Have students volunteer information for the hand diagram while you record the answers on the corresponding finger:
   When: *Once upon a time*
   Where: *in the woods*
   Who: *a little girl*
   What: *met a tricky wolf*
   Why: *because she was taking a shortcut to her grandmother's house.*

5. Demonstrate how to put the information together to write a main-idea statement: *Once upon a time, a little girl met a tricky wolf in the woods as she was going to her grandmother's house.*

6. Distribute a copy of page 29 to each student. Have students complete it using a story the whole class has read.

7. Challenge students to complete the Bonus Box activity.

Give The Main Idea A Hand!

Complete the diagram by filling in the information on each finger.
Use the information to write a main-idea statement.

Who?

Where?

What?

When?

Why?

Now write your main-idea statement.

_____

_____

_____

_____

_____

Bonus Box: On the back of this paper, illustrate your main-idea statement.

How To Extend The Lesson:

• Use the reproducible as a prewriting tool for creative-writing assignments. Each student brainstorms ideas for a story by developing the main idea first. After using the reproducible to outline the story's main idea, the student writes his creative tale.

• Reinforce story elements by reviewing a completed reproducible with your class. Ask students to find the information that describes the character, setting, and plot.

• Have students read copies of a short newspaper article and fill out the reproducible to state the main idea. Ask each student to list additional details of the article on a separate piece of paper. Share the responses to compare the main idea to supporting details.

• Use the reproducible as a follow-up to a video or play performance.

• Emphasize the main idea in a paragraph using the hand diagram. Draw the shape of the hand on the board and ask students to complete it with information from a paragraph they have read together.

Award

YOU DESERVE A HAND FOR FINDING THE MAIN IDEA!

Name _____

Fairy-Tale Facts & Opinions

When using a fairy tale to reinforce facts and opinions, students will learn happily ever after!

Skill: Studying facts and opinions

Estimated Lesson Time: 35 minutes

Teacher Preparation:
1. Duplicate the reproducible on page 33 for each student.
2. Select a fairy tale to read aloud to the class.

Materials:
1 copy of page 33 per student
1 fairy tale

Facts	Opinions
Red is a girl.	Red is careless.
The pig has a hammer.	Pigs are hard workers.
The wolf has big teeth.	The wolf is up to no good.

Introducing The Lesson:

Help students discern the difference between facts and opinions. Record the responses on the board. Ask them to think of fact and opinion statements about themselves.

Steps:

1. Discuss with students the difference between the facts and the opinions.

2. Explain to your students that they are going to hear a fairy tale, and each student will choose a character from the story for a fact and opinion activity.

3. Read a fairy tale aloud to the class.

4. Provide each student with a copy of page 33.

5. Ask each student to choose a character and design a face for the character.

6. Have students write facts and opinions about that character.

7. Challenge students to complete the Bonus Box activity.

Facts	Opinions
I have blue eyes.	My blue eyes are pretty.
I am eight years old.	Eight-year-olds are noisy.
I have freckles.	Freckles are attractive.
I have two brothers.	My brothers are funny.

Name _____   *Fact and opinion*

Fairy-Tale Facts & Opinions

Choose a character from the fairy tale you've read.
Write the character's name and the story title below.
Draw the character's face inside the oval shape.
Then list five facts and five opinions about the character.

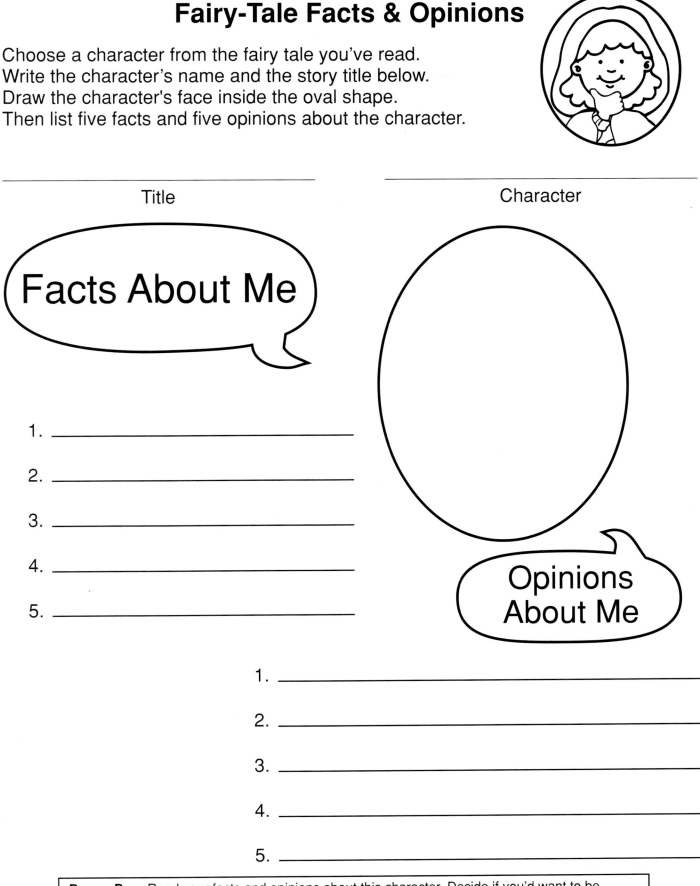

_____   _____
Title   Character

Facts About Me

1. _____

2. _____

3. _____

4. _____

5. _____

Opinions About Me

1. _____

2. _____

3. _____

4. _____

5. _____

Bonus Box: Read your facts and opinions about this character. Decide if you'd want to be friends with this character. Write the reasons on the back of the page.

33

READING

How To Extend The Lesson:

- Ask each student to write five facts and five opinions about himself. Post the resulting lists anonymously and have students attempt to match each list to the person who wrote it.

- Write the names of several famous persons on separate index cards. Tell each student to select a card and ask her to find as many facts and opinions as she can about the famous person.

- Provide each student with a card labeled "fact" and a card labeled "opinion." (See the patterns below.) Make several statements about a story or subject, and ask each student to hold up the appropriate card as the statement is given.

It's a FACT!
It can be proven.

©1997 The Education Center, Inc.

It's an OPINION!
It is a belief or judgement.

©1997 The Education Center, Inc.

34 *Studying facts and opinions*

Catch A Question

Students use comprehension skills to toss around some great ideas in this small-group reading activity.

 Skill: Developing reading comprehension

Estimated Lesson Time: 40 minutes

Teacher Preparation:
1. Duplicate page 37 for each student.
2. Prepare six questions about a story the whole class has read.
3. Write each question on a piece of 8 1/2" by 11" paper, and number each question.

Materials:
1 copy of page 37 per student
6 sheets of 8 1/2" by 11" paper, each programmed with a question

1. Who was the main character?
2. What problem or challenge did the character face?

3. Name three minor characters in the story?
4. How did the ending affect the main character?

5. How was the setting important to the story?
6. Could this story take place in a different time period?

Introducing The Lesson:

Tell students that they are going to work in groups to answer questions about a story they have read. There is an unusual catch to the activity—when each group is through with their question, they toss it to another group, and then catch a new question to answer.

Steps:

1. Distribute a copy of page 37 to each student.

2. Divide students into six groups.

3. Distribute a question to each group and instruct each student to write the group's answer by the corresponding number on the reproducible.

4. After each group has answered the question, give a signal for a member from each group to crumple the paper with the question into a ball and toss it to another group.

5. Each group unfolds the new question and answers it. Repeat the procedure until all six questions have been answered by each group.

6. Challenge students to complete the Bonus Box activity.

Who was the main character?

Catch A Question

Discuss each question with the members of your group.
Write the answer in a complete sentence beside the correct number.

Title Of Story: _____

1. _____ .

_____ .

2. _____ .

_____ .

3. _____ .

_____ .

4. _____ .

_____ .

5. _____ .

_____ .

6. _____ .

_____ .

Bonus Box: On the back of this page, tell three things about your favorite character in the story.

(37)

How To Extend The Lesson:

- Have students write interview questions to ask a character in the story. Select students to role-play the characters during the interviews.

- Ask each group to write a sequel to the story. Have them illustrate the characters to show how they have changed or grown up since the original story.

- Place students into groups to discuss how the story would be different if the time or place of the story were different. Then have each group rewrite the story using a new setting. Share the new stories with the class.

- Have students write the questions for "Catch A Question" when they have finished reading a new story. Provide copies of the form below for students to use in listing their questions.

Name _____

Did you catch the answer to these questions?

1. _____

_____?

2. _____

_____?

3. _____

_____?

Cause-And-Effect Grab Bag

There's no question about it...this bag of tricks will help your students zero in on cause-and-effect situations.

Skill: Identifying cause and effect

Estimated Lesson Time: 35 minutes

Teacher Preparation:
1. Duplicate the reproducible on page 41 for each student.
2. Select a story to read aloud to the class.

Materials:
1 copy of page 41 per student
1 story to read aloud
1 paper bag

It started to rain.

We ran to find shelter.

It was Mary's birthday.

We baked her a cake.

CAUSE

EFFECT

We heard the bell.

We sat down in our seats.

READING

Ribsy

Flat Stanley

The Magic School Bus

The Mitten

Strega Nona

The Talking Eggs

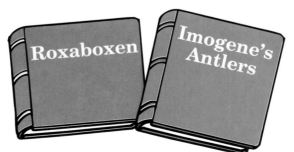

Roxaboxen

Imogene's Antlers

Introducing The Lesson:

Ask students to raise their hands if they have a favorite story. When several students raise their hands, ask them *why* they are holding up their hands. Confirm that the reason is that they are responding to a question. The teacher asked a question, which *caused* students to respond. The *effect* was that the students held up their hands. Instruct students to look for cause-and-effect situations in the upcoming story.

Steps:

1. Select a story and read it aloud to the students, or have the students read the story together.

2. Distribute a copy of page 41 to each student.

3. Have students cut the paper on the dotted lines and fold it in half once, then in half again.

4. Ask each student to write a question asking *why* something happened in the story on the outside of the paper. The student then writes the answer to the question on the inside of the folded paper.

5. Tell each student to put his question inside the paper bag.

6. Have a student select a question and read it to the class. The student with the correct answer may choose the next question to read aloud.

7. Challenge students to complete the Bonus Box activity after all the questions have been selected and answered.

40 *Identifying cause and effect*

Question Grab Bag

After reading a story, write a "why" question and its correct
  answer in the appropriate spaces below.
Cut along the dotted lines.
Fold the paper in half once, then in half again.
Put your question and answer inside the paper bag.

_____

_____

_____

_____

_____

Answer:

Question:

_____

_____

_____

_____

_____

©1997 The Education Center, Inc.

Bonus Box: Use your imagination! Draw illustrations for your question and answer.

How To Extend The Lesson:

- Challenge your students to write sequels to the story. Encourage students to read their stories to the class. Ask students to identify a cause-and-effect situation in each sequel.

- Tell each student to fold a piece of paper in half. Have him draw an event that happened in the story on one side and draw its effect on the other side.

- Create a cause-and-effect Concentration game. Write or draw a cause and its effect on separate index cards. Make several sets of cards. To play, student partners place the cards facedown and take turns selecting two cards at a time in search of a corresponding set.

Ribsy did not come home.

Henry put an ad in the paper.

LOST DOG

A dog that shakes hands with its left paw.

What A Story!

Students combine prediction skills with imagination in this creative-writing activity.

Skill: Predicting outcomes

Estimated Lesson Time: 45 minutes

Teacher Preparation:
Duplicate page 45 for each student.

Materials:
1 copy of page 45 per student

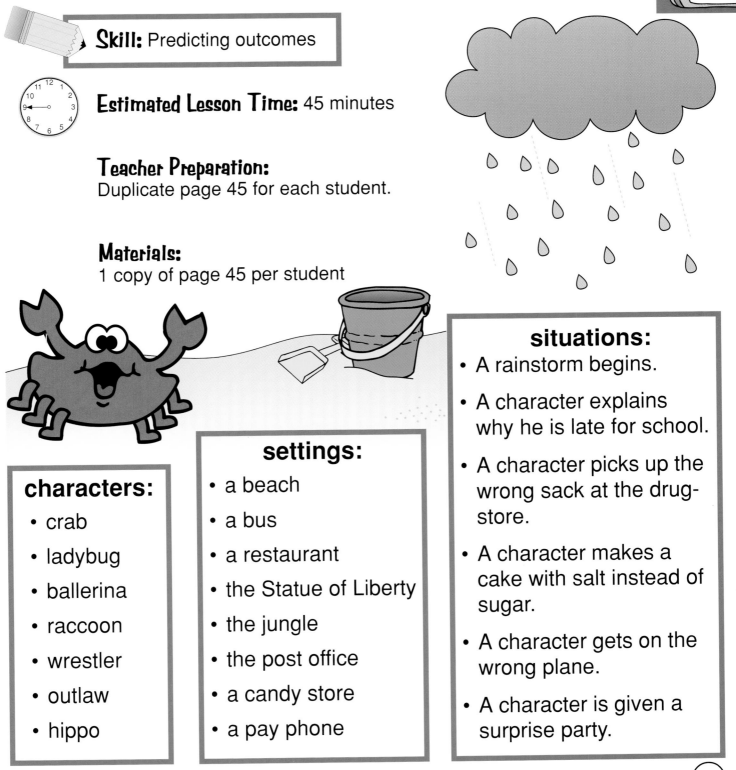

characters:

- crab
- ladybug
- ballerina
- raccoon
- wrestler
- outlaw
- hippo

settings:

- a beach
- a bus
- a restaurant
- the Statue of Liberty
- the jungle
- the post office
- a candy store
- a pay phone

situations:

- A rainstorm begins.
- A character explains why he is late for school.
- A character picks up the wrong sack at the drugstore.
- A character makes a cake with salt instead of sugar.
- A character gets on the wrong plane.
- A character is given a surprise party.

Introducing The Lesson:

Ask students to imagine what might happen if someone brought a pet snake for show-and-tell, and it got loose in the classroom. Have students volunteer their ideas. Tell students that they have just made *predictions* about what could happen. Tell students that they will be making predictions for several different story situations.

Steps:

1. Distribute a copy of page 45 to each student.

2. Provide time for students to make story predictions.

3. Challenge students to complete the Bonus Box activity.

Who would be afraid of the snake?

What could the snake eat?

Where would the snake try to hide?

When did someone notice it was missing?

Why did the snake get loose?

Predicting outcomes

What A Story!

Read each section of story information.
Tell what might happen in the story.

Characters: a grandmother and a gorilla
Setting: the grocery store
Situation: Grandmother has lost her glasses and
   is having trouble reading her shopping list.
What happens? _____

_____

_____

_____

_____

Characters: a snake and a turtle
Setting: a movie theater
Situation: The snake and the turtle are having trouble seeing the movie screen.
What happens? _____

_____

_____

_____

_____

Characters: a cowboy and an opera singer
Setting: a doughnut shop
Situation: The two characters both want the last jelly doughnut.
What happens? _____

_____

_____

_____

_____

Characters: a boy and a kangaroo
Setting: a park
Situation: The boy wants to take the kangaroo home as a pet.
What happens? _____

_____

_____

_____

_____

Bonus Box: Draw a picture to go with each story idea.

How To Extend The Lesson:

- Have student volunteers read their story ideas to the class. Discuss stories with similar ideas. Have students surmise why some stories' ideas contain similar elements.

- Create a writing center with a supply of writing paper and three containers labeled "characters," "settings," and "situations." Fill each container with a supply of index cards programmed with appropriate story information. A student visits the center to draw a card from each container. After reading the information, the student writes a story idea using details from the cards. Provide time for students to share their work with the class.

- Begin reading a story to the class, stopping at a crucial part of the story. Have each student write a few sentences telling what he predicts will happen. Allow student volunteers to share their predictions with the class before you finish reading the story.

- Have students create ideas for characters, settings, and situations. Ask each student to write the information on a copy of the form below, then trade papers with a classmate and write a story idea using the classmate's information. Students then trade papers back to share their ideas with each other.

What could happen with:		
Characters	**Setting**	**Situation**

Dictionary Safari

Lead your students into the deepest, darkest corners of the dictionary to track down more than just definitions.

Skill: Using a dictionary

Estimated Lesson Time: 45 minutes

Teacher Preparation:
1. Duplicate page 49 for each student.
2. Provide a dictionary for each student.

Materials:
1 copy of page 49 per student
1 dictionary per student

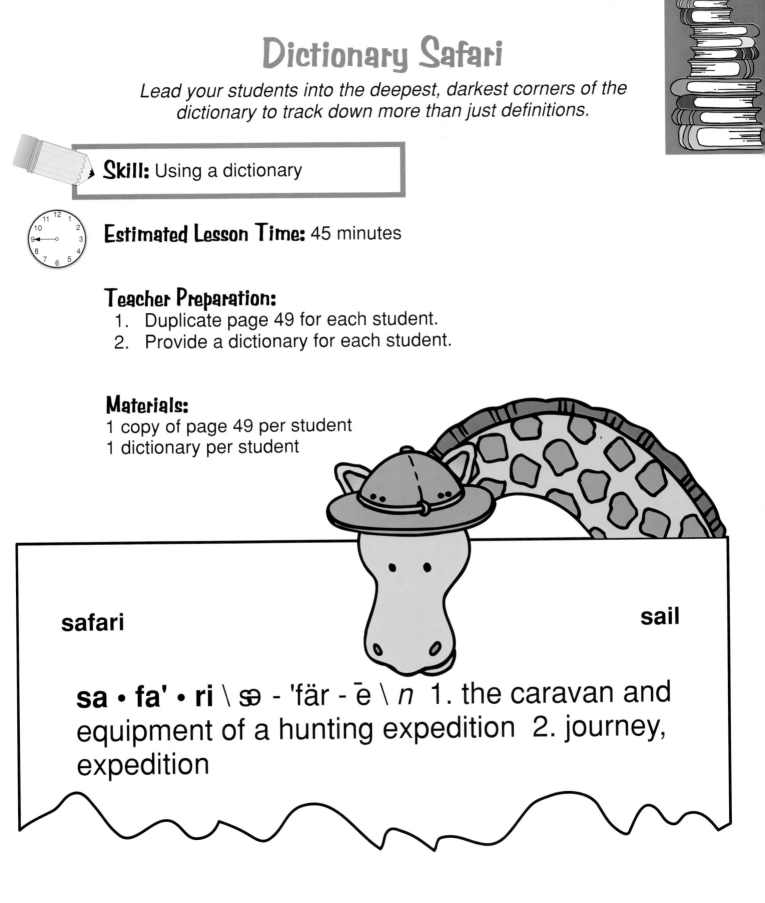

safari

sail

sa • fa' • ri \ sə - 'fär - ē \ *n* 1. the caravan and equipment of a hunting expedition 2. journey, expedition

Introducing The Lesson:

Tell students that they are going to track down some wild, ferocious words. After locating each word, students will capture its meaning on paper and then bag it as a trophy definition.

Steps:

1. Review the term *guide words* and how to use them.

2. Ask students to brainstorm words they consider wild and ferocious, either by the way they sound or by their definitions. List the responses on the board.

3. Distribute a copy of page 49 and a dictionary to each student. Instruct each student to choose two words from the list to use in completing the reproducible.

4. Challenge students to complete the Bonus Box activity.

terrible	bizarre	shocking
fierce	wacky	sensational
reckless	goofy	dreadful
fantastic	strange	incredible
unbelievable	outrageous	gigantic
berserk	disgraceful	tough
frenzy	grizzly	

Dictionary Safari

List the two words you are going to track down.
Then complete the information about each word to capture it on paper.

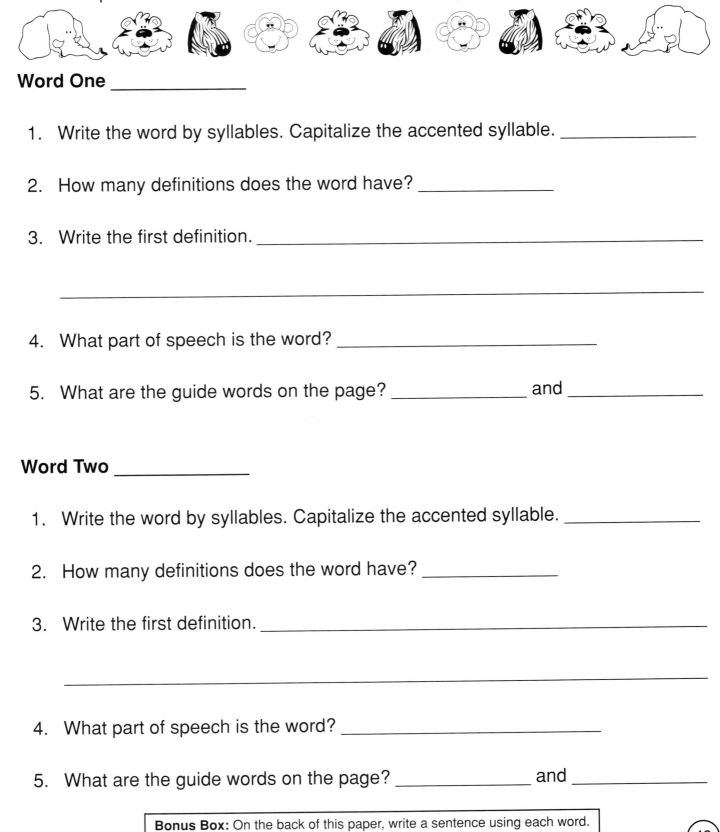

Word One _____

1. Write the word by syllables. Capitalize the accented syllable. _____

2. How many definitions does the word have? _____

3. Write the first definition. _____

_____

4. What part of speech is the word? _____

5. What are the guide words on the page? _____ and _____

Word Two _____

1. Write the word by syllables. Capitalize the accented syllable. _____

2. How many definitions does the word have? _____

3. Write the first definition. _____

_____

4. What part of speech is the word? _____

5. What are the guide words on the page? _____ and _____

Bonus Box: On the back of this paper, write a sentence using each word.

How To Extend The Lesson:

- Use the reproducible for vocabulary development in all content areas. Have students look up words that relate to a science lesson, social-studies concept, or literature theme.

- Introduce a word of the week by writing it on the board and instructing students to find its definition. Give a copy of the award below to each student who uses the word correctly in a sentence during the week.

- Use the reproducible to reinforce word pairs. Give students one word of a pair to use for Word One on the paper, and have them complete the pair by using its synonym, antonym, or homophone for Word Two.

- Play a game to provide practice with guide words and parts of speech. Tell students to find a dictionary page labeled with a specific set of guide words. Then instruct students to look on that page to find an entry word for each category: noun, verb, and adjective. Call on volunteers to announce the entry word, naming its part of speech and definition. Continue playing until every student has volunteered an answer.

CONGRATULATIONS

to _____

for capturing the meaning of a new word.

Word: _____

Meaning: _____

Spin A Story Wheel

*Reinforce literary elements with this spin-off
of the traditional story map.*

Skill: Mapping story elements

Estimated Lesson Time: 30 minutes

Teacher Preparation:
1. Duplicate page 53 for each student.
2. Select a story the class has read.

Materials:
1 copy of page 53 per student

Teacher Reference:

author: the person who wrote the book

character: a person appearing in the story

illustrator: the person who created the pictures in the book

plot: the structure of a story, including the problems or challenges
that a character faces in the story line

setting: where the story takes place

title: the name of the book

Introducing The Lesson:

Tell students that they will be using information from the selected story to complete a story wheel. To get things rolling, have each student stand up and tell one thing about the story, such as a plot detail, a character, or an emotional response he had to the story.

Steps:

1. Provide time for students to discuss their reactions to the story.

2. Distribute page 53 to each student.

3. Challenge students to complete the Bonus Box activity.

Who was your favorite character?

Where did the story take place?

Which character was mentioned first?

Did the setting of the story change?

Who was the most important character?

What problem occurred?

How was the problem solved?

Which character are you most like?

Which character are you least like?

What was your favorite part of the story?

Name _____ *Story elements*

Story Wheel

Complete the wheel with information from the story.
Then write a sentence about the story around the
outline of the wheel.

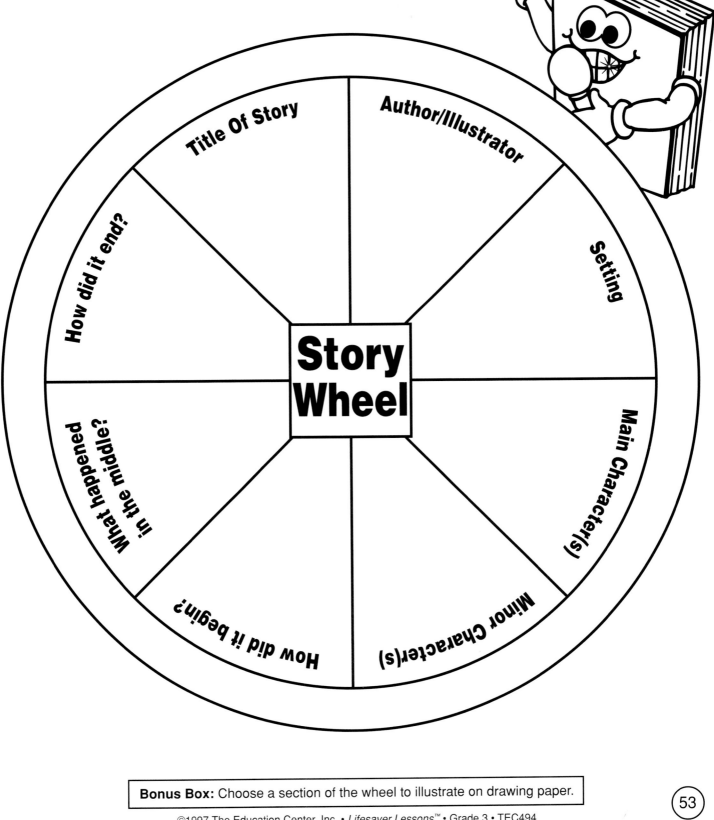

Bonus Box: Choose a section of the wheel to illustrate on drawing paper.

©1997 The Education Center, Inc. • *Lifesaver Lessons*™ • Grade 3 • TEC494

How To Extend The Lesson:

• Have each student select a character from the story. Ask her to imagine what it might be like to spend the day with that character. Instruct each student to write a paragraph telling about the imagined day.

• Let the setting of the book inspire an art activity. Have each student select a scene from the story to illustrate using watercolors or colored chalk.

• Use the Story Wheel for a cooperative-learning activity. Divide students into eight groups. Assign a section of the Story Wheel to each group. Have all the groups record their information on one enlarged copy of the wheel; then display the finished product.

• Use the Story Wheel as a book-report form. Allow each student to select a book to read. After she has read the book, have her complete the Story Wheel form, then share it with the class.

• Provide each student with a copy of the bookmark pattern below. Have the student track his reading progress by listing each book he reads.

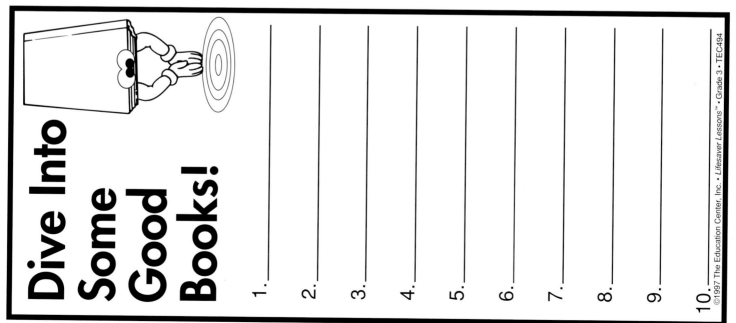

Dive Into Some Good Books!

1.
2.
3.
4.
5.
6.
7.
8.
9.
10.

©1997 The Education Center, Inc. • *Lifesaver Lessons*™ • Grade 3 • TEC494

Picture-Perfect Grammar

Nouns and verbs abound in this picture-related grammar search for these parts of speech.

Skill: Identifying nouns and verbs

Estimated Lesson Time: 30 minutes

Teacher Preparation:
1. Duplicate page 57 for each student.
2. Gather the materials listed below.

Materials:
1 copy of page 57 per student
crayons (optional)

Teacher Reference:
Common nouns indicate a class of persons, places, and things. (girl, city, car)

Pronouns take the place of nouns. (I, you, he)

Proper nouns name a particular person, place, or thing. (Andy, Arizona, Coke®)

Verbs are words that show action, state of being, or occurance.

Linking verbs are followed by a word or phrase that modifies the subject of a sentence. (Randy *is* tall.)

Introducing The Lesson:

Ask each student to look around the room and inconspicuously observe one of his classmates. Instruct the student to notice five things about the classmate. After a given time, ask students to volunteer their observations while you list them on the board. When the responses have been recorded, ask students to categorize them into naming words and action words.

Steps:

1. Reinforce for students the fact that naming words are called *nouns* and that action words are called *verbs*.

2. Distribute a copy of page 57 to each student.

3. Provide time for students to observe the picture and create lists of nouns and verbs. If time allows, have students color the picture.

4. Challenge students to complete the Bonus Box activity.

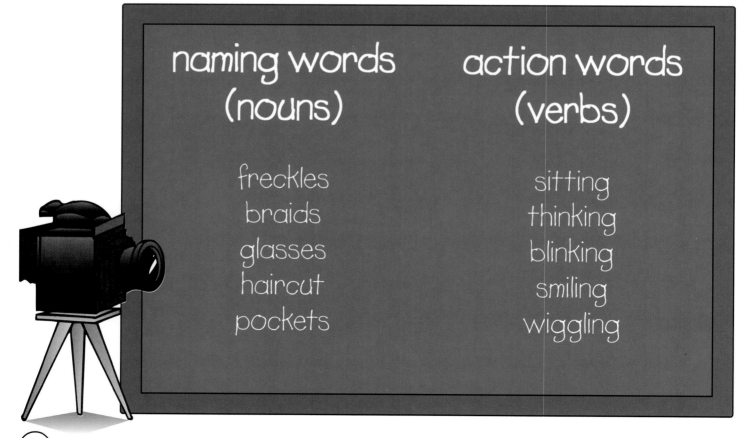

naming words (nouns)	action words (verbs)
freckles	sitting
braids	thinking
glasses	blinking
haircut	smiling
pockets	wiggling

Picture-Perfect Grammar

Look at the picture.
List examples of nouns and verbs shown in the picture.

Nouns   Verbs

_____ _____   _____ _____

_____ _____   _____ _____

_____ _____   _____ _____

_____ _____   _____ _____

_____ _____   _____ _____

Bonus Box: On the back of the paper, list five nouns and verbs that are *not* in the picture.

How To Extend The Lesson:

• If weather permits, take students outdoors to observe children on your school playground. Challenge them to find a predetermined amount of nouns and verbs as they observe the playground scene.

• Place students in small groups. Distribute a copy of the same picture to each group. (If desired, use the example shown below.) Have each group try to find as many examples of nouns and verbs as possible in the picture, and then record them in a list. After a certain amount of time, ask for a total number from each group; then check the word lists together.

• Have students look through old magazines for pictures that contain examples of nouns and verbs. Have them work individually or with partners to create lists for their pictures.

• Reverse the lesson by giving the students a list of nouns and verbs and then having them create pictures showing examples of the words. Provide time for students to show their pictures to the class.

• Have students brainstorm nouns and verbs associated with the current holiday or season. Give each student a sheet of drawing paper to illustrate and label the nouns and verbs.

Absolutely Adjectives

Lead your students on a mission for description, and watch some awesome adjectives appear!

Skill: Using adjectives

Estimated Lesson Time: 30 minutes

Teacher Preparation:

1. Duplicate page 61 for each student.
2. Gather the materials listed below.

Materials:

1 copy of page 61 per student
1 self-stick note per student

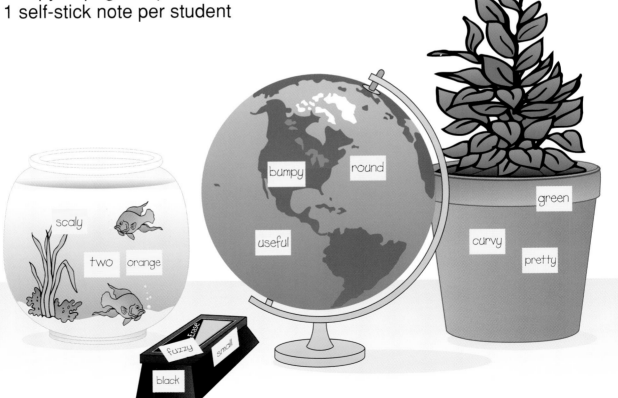

Introducing The Lesson:

Tell students to look around the room and notice signs of description. Remind students that description words, or adjectives, can tell about size, shape, color, number, or a certain quality of an object. After students have observed the classroom for several minutes, distribute a self-stick note to each student. Instruct the student to pick out an object and write a describing word for it on the note. Then have each student attach her note to the object it describes.

Steps:

1. After students return to their desks, walk around the room and read the notes aloud.

2. Ask students to identify each adjective as one describing size, shape, color, number, or a certain quality.

3. Tell students that they are going to continue making observations about descriptions as they complete the information on the reproducible.

4. Challenge students to complete the Bonus Box activity.

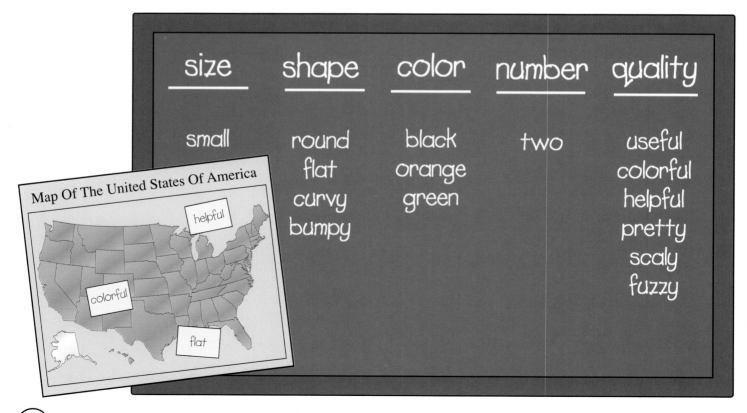

size	shape	color	number	quality
small	round	black	two	useful
	flat	orange		colorful
	curvy	green		helpful
	bumpy			pretty
				scaly
				fuzzy

Map Of The United States Of America

helpful

colorful

flat

Absolutely Adjectives

List ten objects that you see in the room.
Then write adjectives that describe each object.

Objects	Description Words
1. _____	_____
2. _____	_____
3. _____	_____
4. _____	_____
5. _____	_____
6. _____	_____
7. _____	_____
8. _____	_____
9. _____	_____
10. _____	_____

Choose three of the objects on your list.
Write a descriptive sentence about each object.

1. _____

2. _____

3. _____

Bonus Box: On the back of the paper, list the senses you used in describing the objects.

©1997 The Education Center, Inc. • *Lifesaver Lessons*™ • Grade 3 • TEC494

How To Extend The Lesson:

- Have students compare the objects they described. List the adjectives used for a common object. As a class, compose a paragraph using all the descriptions students listed for that object.

- Have students use the information on their reproducibles for a descriptive writing assignment. Then supply each student with a piece of drawing paper to illustrate his description.

- Incorporate art appreciation into a reinforcement activity by displaying a copy of a famous work of art and having each student list ten adjectives to describe it. Discuss the words on the lists to explore students' reactions to the art.

- Place students in cooperative groups and challenge each group to list as many adjectives as possible to describe a topic, such as ice cream or feathers. Compare the lists as a review of descriptive word choices.

- Introduce an adjective a day by writing an unusual or unfamiliar adjective on the board. Have students find the word in the dictionary. Challenge the students to use the word at least twice during the day.

droll	savory	elaborate
corpulent	sluggish	humdrum
loquacious	mischievous	beneficial
blissful	tranquil	jubilant
tedious	skittish	sullen
petite	hideous	irascible
ample	wretched	peevish
perilous	outlandish	enthralling

Sentence Shenanigans

Tickle your students' funny bones with this light-hearted look at sentence structure.

Skill: Identifying subjects and predicates

Estimated Lesson Time: 45 minutes

Teacher Preparation:
1. Duplicate page 65 for each student.
2. Obtain an example of items commonly paired together (see materials).

Materials:
1 copy of page 65 per student
an example of items commonly paired together, such as peanut butter and jelly, macaroni and cheese, or a hammer and nail

Background Information:
- A subject consists of the main noun (or a group of words acting as the main noun) and tells what the sentence is about.

- A predicate contains a verb and sometimes a group of words related to the verb. It describes something about the subject.

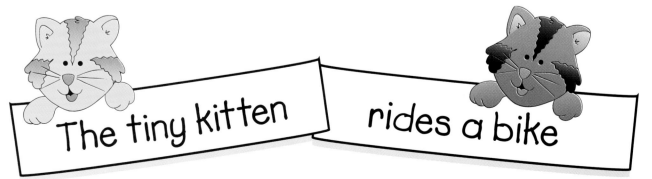

The tiny kitten   rides a bike

Introducing The Lesson:

Show students an example of items that are commonly paired together. Ask students to name some other items that create pairs. List their responses on the board. Remind students that a sentence is made up of a very important pair: a *subject* and a *predicate.* Review the definitions of subject and predicate with your students. Tell the class that they will be pairing together an assortment of subjects and predicates to come up with some interesting and unusual sentences.

Steps:

1. Distribute a copy of page 65 to each student.

2. Instruct students to compose subjects and predicates in the appropriate sections of the reproducible, then cut apart the completed sections.

3. Gather the sections and place in two stacks, one for subjects and one for predicates.

4. Ask a student volunteer to draw a section from each stack, then write the two sections on the board as a complete sentence. Direct the student to read the sentence to the class, then identify the subject and the predicate in the sentence.

5. Continue the activity until each student has had a turn, or as time allows.

6. Challenge students to complete the Bonus Box activity.

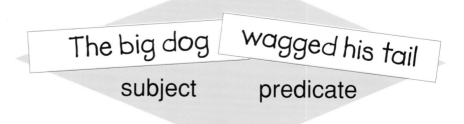

The big dog | wagged his tail

subject   predicate

Sentence Shenanigans

Write the subject of a sentence in each box, and then cut apart. Example:

The tiny kitten

Subject
Subject
Subject

Write the predicate of a sentence in each box, and then cut apart. Example:

rides a bike

Predicate
Predicate
Predicate

Follow your teacher's directions to make sentences with the subjects and predicates.

Bonus Box: Draw a picture to illustrate one of the completed sentences.

How To Extend The Lesson:

- Have students work in pairs to compose a list of ten subjects and a list of ten predicates. Have each student pair trade its subject list with another pair of students. Instruct each pair to use the new subject list and the predicate list to create ten sentences. Provide time for each pair to read a few of the sentences to the class.

- Select a student each day to be the Official Daily Subject. Have the class use the student's name as the subject in sentence-writing practice.

- Ask students to brainstorm a list of predicates that describe things the students do in the course of a school day. Have each student write one of the predicates on a sentence strip. Post the completed strips on a bulletin board with the subject "Third-Grade Students…"

- Divide the class into two teams for a game of subject-and-predicate baseball. The team who is "at bat" stands in a line while the other team's members stay at their desks to await their turn at bat. "Pitch" a sentence to the first player in line. The student listens to the sentence, then must identify the subject (or predicate) of the sentence. If he is correct, he walks to a desk designated as first base. (Also designate a second base, third base, and home plate.) If he is incorrect, he sits down at his desk to indicate an "out." Play continues as the next player in line repeats the routine. Award a point for each player that makes it back to home plate. Call the second team to bat when the first team has earned three outs.

Third-Grade Students…

learn multiplication facts.

go to lunch at 11:45.

play baseball at recess.

know the order of the planets.

study insects.

take spelling tests.

can use calculators.

love school.

It's In The Bag!

Encourage creative thinking with this story starter that provides an unlimited flow of ideas.

Skill: Practicing creative writing

Estimated Lesson Time: 45 minutes

Teacher Preparation:
1. Duplicate page 69 for each student.
2. Place three or four small, varied objects in a paper bag. (The objects can be an assortment of unrelated items, such as a gum wrapper, a comb, a magnifying glass, and a marble.)

Materials:
1 copy of page 69 per student
1 paper bag containing several small objects

Introducing The Lesson:

Tell students that you have a bag with a big story in it. Explain that the bag contains several objects that relate to the story. Take the objects from the bag one by one, allowing the class to observe and comment on each item.

Steps:

1. After students have observed the contents of the bag, distribute a copy of page 69 to each student and tell him to write a story that includes the objects in the story line.

2. Challenge students to complete the Bonus Box activity.

Who are the characters?

Where does the story take place?

How is each object important to the story?

Name _____

It's In The Bag!

List the objects in the bag. Then write a story about the objects.

Objects: _____   _____   _____   _____

Bonus Box: Give your story a title. Then draw a picture of one of the objects from the story.

How To Extend The Lesson:

- Provide time for students to share their stories from page 69 with the class. Then have students categorize their stories into genres such as mystery, humor, fantasy, realistic fiction, and science fiction.

- Have students illustrate their stories by drawing with crayon on paper lunch sacks. Display the pictures and stories on a bulletin board titled "The Story Is In The Bag."

- Ask for student volunteers to bring bags of objects from home. Place the bags in a center and let students choose one to write about.

- After reading a story as a class, have students create a bag of items that relate to the story. Send an empty bag home with each student to fill with several items that are significant to the story.

THE STORY IS IN THE BAG

Lunar Letters

Neither rain, nor sleet, nor dark of night, will stop your students from learning letter-writing skills!

Skill: Writing a friendly letter

Estimated Lesson Time: 30 minutes

Teacher Preparation:

1. Duplicate page 73 for each student.
2. Write the model of a friendly letter from page 72 on the board.

Materials:

1 copy of page 73 per student

Background Information:

The parts of a friendly letter are:

- *heading:* includes the sender's address and the date the letter was written
- *greeting:* tells to whom the letter was written
- *body:* tells what the letter is about
- *closing:* brings the letter to a close
- *signature:* tells who wrote the letter

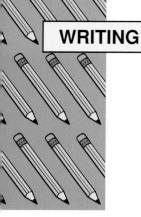

Introducing The Lesson:

Tell your students to imagine that they have the opportunity to go on an amazing field trip to the moon! The only catch is that they have to leave shortly, and will not have time to talk to their parents before they go. Have each student write a letter to her parents explaining the situation.

Steps:

1. Write the sample letter below on the board showing students the five parts of a friendly letter.

2. Distribute a copy of page 73 to each student.

3. Challenge students to complete the Bonus Box activity.

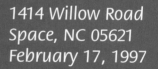

1414 Willow Road
Space, NC 05621
February 17, 1997

Dear Students,

We have a wonderful opportunity! We have been invited on a field trip to the moon. We must board the rocket very soon, but we need to let our parents know where we are. Please write a letter to them explaining the situation.

Your teacher,
Mrs. Blastoff

☆ Lunar Letters

_____

_____

_____

_____

_____

_____

_____

_____

_____

_____

_____

_____

_____

Bonus Box: On the back of the paper, design a stamp to illustrate the contents of your letter.

©1997 The Education Center, Inc. • *Lifesaver Lessons*™ • Grade 3 • TEC494

73

How To Extend This Lesson:

- Have each student write another letter to show how he thinks his parents would respond to the field-trip letter.

- Have each student write a letter telling about his field trip to the moon.

- Find a company for the children to write to asking for a pamphlet, a sample, or some other information. Show the children how to correctly address an envelope with their return addresses and the company's address.

- If possible, arrange a field trip to a post office. Let students see how the mail is sorted for delivery.

- Ask students to bring postmarked envelopes from mail they have received at home. Place the envelopes in a center with a large map. Have students use the map to locate the origins of each postmark.

- Share a story that focuses on letter writing. *The Jolly Postman: Or Other People's Letters* by Janet and Allan Ahlberg (Little, Brown and Company; 1986) follows a postman through the land of fairy tales, and lets you peek inside some very interesting envelopes!

Paragraph-Writing Recipe

When students follow this basic recipe for paragraph writing, they will get gourmet results!

Skill: Writing a paragraph

Estimated Lesson Time: 30 minutes

Teacher Preparation:
1. Duplicate page 77 for each student.
2. Provide a class supply of cookies.

Materials:
1 copy of page 77 per student
1 cookie per student

Cook up a paragraph
with these tasty topics:
• your favorite sport
• a famous person
• a hobby
• a science concept
• social studies information
• a holiday
• a book or movie character

Writing a paragraph 75

Introducing The Lesson:

Begin your lesson by distributing a cookie to each student. Tell students to take a bite; then have them list some of the ingredients typically found in cookies. After naming possible ingredients, discuss the steps that are followed when baking cookies.

Steps:

1. Tell student that they will follow a recipe to "cook up" a paragraph. They will have to gather the necessary ingredients, then follow the steps for putting the paragraph together.

2. Distribute a copy of page 77 to each student.

3. Challenge students to complete the Bonus Box activity.

sugar
butter
flour
vanilla
chocolate chips

1. Preheat the oven.
2. Mix the ingredients.
3. Drop spoonfuls onto a cookie sheet.
4. Bake in the oven.
5. Cool on a wire rack.

Recipe For A Red-Hot Paragraph

Gather the ingredients listed below.
Then follow the steps to complete the paragraph.

Ingredients:

• one topic:_____

• explain how you know about the topic: _____

_____

• two facts about the topic:

_____

_____

• an opinion about the topic:

_____

Steps:

1. Begin with a sentence announcing the topic. Write it below.
2. Follow with a sentence explaining how you know about the topic.
3. Take one fact and write a sentence with it.
4. Add another sentence with the second fact.
5. Supply an opinion about the topic for a finishing touch.

_____

_____

_____

_____

_____

_____

Bonus Box: Proofread your paragraph. Underline your topic sentence with a blue crayon. Highlight each capital letter with a yellow crayon. Highlight each punctuation mark with a red crayon.

How To Extend The Lesson:

- Have each student read his paragraph from page 77 to the class. After each student reads, have him state the main idea of the paragraph.

- Use the recipe format as a science or social studies review. Assign a topic from either subject for students to explain in paragraph form.

- Incorporate show-and-tell with paragraph writing. Ask each student to write a paragraph about the object he would like to present. Have him read his paragraph to tell about the object he shows to the class.

- Have students write a paragraph as a cooperative group activity. Place students in groups of five. Tell each student in the group to write one of the sentences for the paragraph. Have each group present its completed paragraph to the class.

- Write each sentence of a paragraph on a separate sentence strip. Have students place the strips in logical order to form a paragraph.

- Have students prepare a batch of No-Bake Nibbles. After each student samples the treat, instruct her to write a paragraph about her favorite snack.

No-Bake Nibbles

You will need:
1 cup honey
1 1/2 cups powdered milk
1 1/2 cups wheat germ
1/2 cup raisins
1/2 cup chocolate chips
Combine all ingredients together.
Shape into small balls.
Eat and enjoy!

Looking Into The Future

Travel on a futuristic journey as penned through your students' descriptive writing.

Skill: Practicing descriptive writing

Estimated Lesson Time: 45 minutes

Teacher Preparation:
1. Duplicate page 81 for each student.
2. Gather the materials listed below.

Materials:
1 copy of page 81 per student
1 sheet of 6 3/4" x 9" blank paper per student

Clothing

Entertainment

Occupations

Transportation

Introducing The Lesson:

Tell students that their writing assignment involves a time travel adventure to the past and then to the future. Ask students to imagine what their lives would have been like 100 years ago. Tell them to think about styles in clothing, methods of transportation, forms of entertainment, and types of occupations from the past and compare them to what we have today. Record students' responses on the board. Next tell students to use their imaginations to predict what the future will bring for each of those categories. Explain that they will use their predictions to create a futuristic magazine.

Steps:

1. Provide each student with a copy of page 81 and one sheet of blank paper.

2. Instruct the student to cut out the cover and fold it on the thin line. Then fold the blank page in half.

3. Have students insert the folded blank page into the cover and staple them together on the left-hand side to form the magazine.

4. Tell students to fill in the blanks for the date and name, then label each blank page with one of the following titles: Clothing, Transportation, Entertainment, and Occupations.

5. Instruct students to illustrate each page with items from the future, then write a descriptive paragraph under each illustration.

6. Have each student complete the information on the back cover.

7. Provide time for students to share their completed magazines with the class.

Looking Into The Future

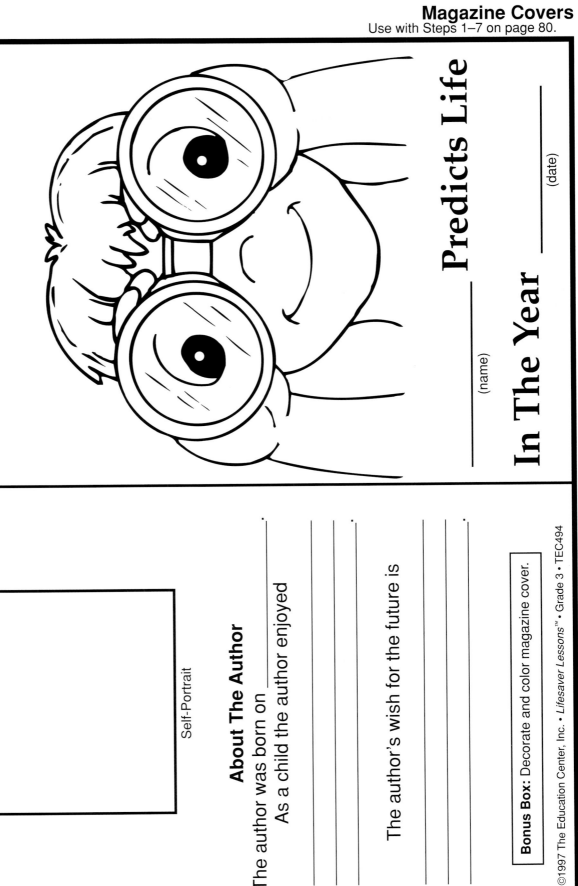

Predicts Life

_____
(name)

In The Year

_____
(date)

Self-Portrait

About The Author

The author was born on _____

As a child the author enjoyed _____

_____

_____

The author's wish for the future is _____

_____

_____

Bonus Box: Decorate and color magazine cover.

How To Extend The Lesson:

- Encourage students to add pages to their magazines describing other topics for the future.

- Invite students to create and wear their own future fashions. Then host a fashion show of the future.

- Instruct each student to write about something he hopes will not be changed in the future. Ask volunteers to share their papers with the class.

- Create a bulletin board using cutouts of students' handprints traced on colored construction paper. Have each student trace his hand, cut out the resulting shape, and write a sentence on the shape describing a hope he has for the future. Arrange the cutouts on the bulletin board and add the title "The Future Is In Our Hands."

Couplet Capers

*A poetry lesson will be so inviting
when students use rhyming words in their writing.*

Skill: Identifying rhyming words

Estimated Lesson Time: 30 minutes

Teacher Preparation:
1. Duplicate page 85 for each student.
2. Copy the couplet poem below onto the board.

Materials:
1 copy of page 85 for each student

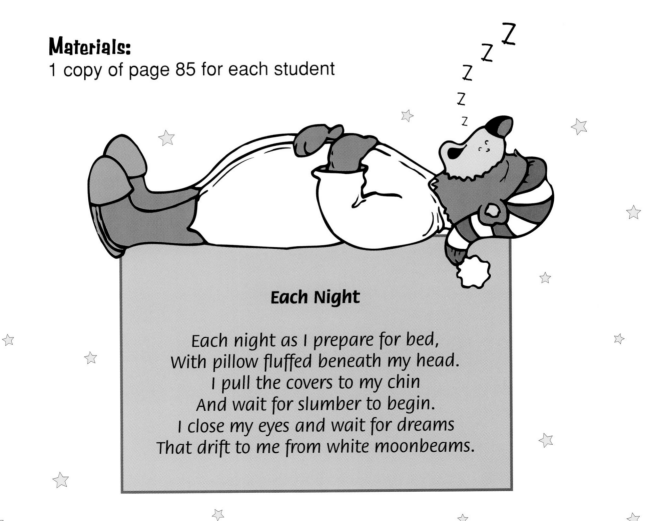

Each Night

Each night as I prepare for bed,
With pillow fluffed beneath my head.
I pull the covers to my chin
And wait for slumber to begin.
I close my eyes and wait for dreams
That drift to me from white moonbeams.

Introducing The Lesson:

Direct student's attention to the poem you have written on the board. Read it to them; then have the class repeat it as a choral reading.

Ask students to locate the rhyming words in the poem. Explain that poetry can be written in couplets, with rhyming words at the end of each pair of lines. Tell the students that they will be creating word lists of rhyming words, then writing couplets with words from their lists.

Steps:

1. Distribute a copy of page 85 to each student.

2. Help students brainstorm words for the word boxes.

3. Allow time for students to create couplets using words from the word boxes.

4. Challenge students to complete the Bonus Box activity.

bed
head

chin
begin

dreams
moonbeams

Identifying rhyming words

Name _____

Rhyme Time

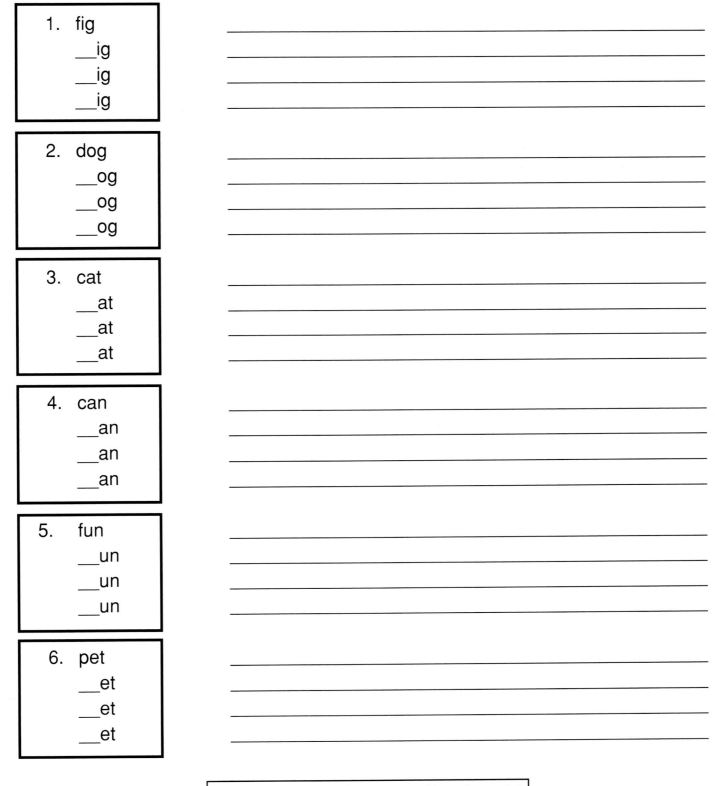

Write a list of rhyming words in each word box.
Then write a couplet with a word pair from each box.

1. fig
   __ig
   __ig
   __ig

2. dog
   __og
   __og
   __og

3. cat
   __at
   __at
   __at

4. can
   __an
   __an
   __an

5. fun
   __un
   __un
   __un

6. pet
   __et
   __et
   __et

Bonus Box: Draw a picture to go with each couplet.

How To Extend The Lesson:

• Have students read their couplets from page 85 to the class. Ask students to identify the rhyming words in each couplet.

• Give each student a copy of a poem and have him circle the rhyming words at the ends of the lines.

• Prepare one line of a couplet and write it on the board. Have each student copy the line in her best handwriting, then create a second line for the couplet. Display the finished couplets on a bulletin board.

• Share some of the rhyming books below with your students. Have students identify the rhyming words as you read the poems to them.

—*Hand Rhymes* by Marc Brown (Dutton Children's Books, 1985)

—*The Ice Cream Store* by Dennis Lee (Scholastic Inc., 1992)

—*Rhymes For Annie Rose* by Shirley Hughes (Lothrop, Lee and Shepard; 1995)

—*Walking The Bridge Of Your Nose* by Michael Rosen (Kingfisher, 1995)

—*What To Do When A Bug Climbs In Your Mouth And Other Poems To Drive You Buggy* by Rick Walton (Lothrop, Lee and Shepard; 1995)

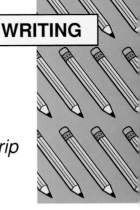

Creative Comic Strips

Move over Garfield®! Students can create their own comic strip with this unique way to write a book report!

Skill: Creating a book report

Estimated Lesson Time: 40 minutes

Teacher Preparation:

1. Duplicate page 89 for each student.
2. Select a book for students to read.
3. If desired, make an overhead transparency of a comic strip.

Materials:

1 copy of page 89 per student

a selected book

overhead of a comic strip, if desired

Tom Cat took a survey of everyone's favorite dessert.

The most popular answer was a "mice-cream" cone.

They say that the colder the mouse, the cooler the cat.

Introducing The Lesson:

Show students an overhead transparency of a comic strip, or ask students if they have ever seen a comic strip in the funny papers. Have students describe a comic strip, making sure that they mention the different frames in the comic strip, the dialogue balloons or captions, and the sequenced events. Ask students to help you generate a cartoon on the board showing a student getting ready for school. Draw a comic strip with several frames on the board; then have students supply ideas for sequencing a character in the process of getting ready for school. Tell students they will use this comic-strip format to create a book report.

Steps:

1. Read a book with the class.
2. Discuss the sequence of events from the story.
3. Provide each student with a copy of page 89.
4. Ask each student to use the comic strip to summarize the story.
5. Remind students that each frame should be in sequential order.
6. Tell students to include an illustration and caption for each frame.
7. Challenge students to complete the Bonus Box activity.

Creative Comic Strips

Write a book report using the comic-strip format.
Show a scene from the story in each frame and include a caption.
Don't forget to sequence your comic strip from beginning to end!

1	2	3
Title:_____ Author:_____		
4	5	6

Bonus Box: On the back of the page, draw your own creative comic character. Write a comic strip featuring your character.

©1997 The Education Center, Inc. • *Lifesaver Lessons*™ • Grade 3 • TEC494

How To Extend The Lesson:

- Cut a comic strip out of the newspaper. Use liquid paper to delete the words. Post the comic strip in your writing center and have students create new dialogue.

- Tell students to select a book to read independently, then create a comic-strip book report about this story. Place the books and comic strips in a center. Challenge the class to match the resulting comic strips to the original books.

- Have each student select a character from a book, then make a comic strip of that character in a new situation.

- Bring in actual comic strips from the newspaper. Have each student select one and write a story using the same sequence of events as shown in the comic-strip frames.

- Have the students work in pairs to create a comic strip about a book they have read together. Display the completed projects on a bulletin board covered with a newspaper background.

Ready, Set, Edit!

Capitalize on this unusual story starter to promote students' editing skills.

Skill: Editing

Estimated Lesson Time: 40 minutes

Teacher Preparation:
Duplicate page 93 for each student.

Materials:
1 copy of page 93 per student

Topic List

holidays
animals
recycling
favorite books
types of music
plants
desserts
games
school subjects
types of shoes

Introducing The Lesson:

Ask students to stand up and turn their desks around so that they are facing the opposite direction. Have students sit down in this new arrangement. Ask for their reactions to the new arrangement. Then have students imagine what it would be like if their school day happened in the opposite order. Ask for several ideas; then tell students to use those ideas (as well as any others they may have) to complete a writing and editing assignment.

Steps:

1. Distribute a copy of page 93 to each student.

2. Ask each student to write down on the reproducible the topic of the assignment and three ideas relating to the topic.

3. Have students refer to their three ideas as they write a story on a separate sheet of paper.

4. Instruct students to edit their completed work using the form on the reproducible.

5. Have students make any necessary corrections.

6. Challenge students to complete the Bonus Box activity.

Name _____

Ready, Set, Edit!

Use this outline to help you think of ideas for your writing.
Then edit your work with the form below.

My topic: _____

Idea for paragraph one: _____
_____

Idea for paragraph two: _____
_____

Idea for paragraph three: _____
_____

Editing My Work	Yes	No
I used each one of the ideas in a paragraph.		
I indented the first word of each paragraph.		
I used the correct punctuation at the end of each sentence.		
I used a capital letter at the beginning of each sentence.		
I checked for spelling mistakes.		
I used neat handwriting.		

Bonus Box: Trade papers with a friend. Proofread each other's work.

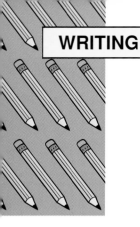
How To Extend The Lesson:

• Provide a teacher-created writing sample that contains several errors. Have students use the checklist on page 93 to help spot the errors, then rewrite the sample correctly.

• Show students some basic proofreading marks as shown on the chart below. Practice using the marks with a writing sample copied onto an overhead transparency. Have student volunteers show how to use the marks as the class edits the writing sample together.

• Use the reproducible on page 93 with other writing topics. If desired, use the activity once a week to reinforce proofreading and editing skills.

• Keep and date several writing samples for each student in individual portfolios. Each grading period, have students look over their writing samples and evaluate their progress.

Proofreading Marks

Instruction	Mark In Margin	Mark In Text	Corrected Text
delete	ℓ	the ~~bad~~ dog	the dog
make capital	(cap)	the dog	The dog
make lowercase	(lc)	the Ɗog	the dog
spell out	(sp)	(2) dogs	two dogs
insert comma	⌃	dogs dogs dogs	dogs, dogs, dogs
insert period	⊙	See the dogs⊙	See the dogs.
start paragraph	¶	"Do you see the dog?"¶ "I don't see it."	"Do you see the dog?" "I don't see it."

Answer Keys

Page 5

smart	enclose
smear	engine
smile	enjoy
smoke	enough
smudge	enter
grape	class
great	clever
grill	climb
growl	cloud
grudge	club

black
blend
blind
blow
blush

Page 13

1. Dr. = Doctor
2. Jr. = Junior
3. U.S.A. = United States of America
4. Tues. = Tuesday
5. Jan. = January
6. 1st = first
7. E.R. = Emergency Room
8. St. = Street
9. Rd. = Road
10. 3rd = third

Page 21

The word listed first by each number should be circled on the student's paper.

1. sum, some
2. sun, son
3. write, right
4. bear, bare
5. deer, dear
6. flower, flour
7. wood, would
8. nose, knows
9. hare, hair

Notes

Grade 3 Language Arts Management Check List

SKILLS	PAGES	DATE(S) USED	COMMENTS
WORD SKILLS			
Alphabetizing	3		
Suffixes	7		
Abbreviations	11		
Antonyms	15		
Homophones	19		
READING			
Following Directions	23		
Main Idea	27		
Fact And Opinion	31		
Comprehension	35		
Cause And Effect	39		
Predicting Outcomes	43		
Dictionary Skills	47		
Story Elements	51		
GRAMMAR			
Nouns And Verbs	55		
Adjectives	59		
Subjects And Predicates	63		
WRITING			
Creative Writing	67		
Friendly Letters	71		
Paragraph Writing	75		
Descriptive Writing	79		
Poetry	83		
Book Reports	87		
Editing	91		